May - June '94

Life as you know it
is about to end ....

good luck!

Hank + Vicki

IF WE'D WANTED QUIET, WE WOULD HAVE RAISED GOLDFISH

Poems for Parents

Selected by **Bruce Lansky**

Meadowbrook Press
Distributed by Simon & Schuster
New York

Library of Congress Cataloging-in-Publication Data

If we'd wanted quiet, we would have raised goldfish: poems for parents / selected by
    Bruce Lansky.
        p.   cm.
    1.   Parent and child—Poetry.   2. Parenting—Poetry.   3. Children—
    Poetry.   4. American poetry.   I. Lansky, Bruce.
    PS595.P37I35   1994
    811.008'0352083—dc20   94–807
                                                                                  CIP

Editor: Bruce Lansky
Submissions Editor: Craig Hansen
Photo Editor: David Tobey
Managing Editor: Dale E. Howard
Production Manager: Amy Unger
Desktop Prepress Manager: Jon C. Wright
Designer: Erik Broberg
Cover photography: Bill Gale Photography, Inc., Minneapolis

ISBN: 0-88166-210-0
Simon & Schuster Ordering #: 0-671-89457-9

Published by Meadowbrook Press, 18318 Minnetonka Boulevard,
Deephaven, MN 55391.

BOOK TRADE DISTRIBUTION by Simon & Schuster, a division of Simon and
Schuster, Inc., 1230 Avenue of the Americas, New York, NY 10020

99 98 97 96 95 94   10 9 8 7 6 5 4 3 2 1

Printed in the United States of America

Contents

Introduction

$\mathcal{I}$f you're a parent, or expecting to become one, I think you'll enjoy this book—even if you haven't picked up a book of poetry since you left school. I've carefully selected poems that communicate, rather than obscure, the emotional experiences of the authors. Some of the poems will make you laugh; others may bring tears. But they all are a pleasure to read.

Poetry uses words to paint pictures. The poems in this book capture, in images that enable you to see, smell, hear, touch, and feel—to share in—the most poignant moments of parenthood, from conception to children caring for their aging parents.

Here are some of the word-pictures that have stuck, indelibly, in my mind:

Laurie Lico Albanese captures the joyful moment of conception in "Dancing Baby."

> *I felt you dance into me.*

Margaret Park Bridges, in "Moved," describes a reflective moment shared with her baby.

> *I feed on her now.*
> *She yawns, and as her eyes open,*
> *she spoons a smile into my hungry heart*
> *where it warms me like no oven.*

Charles David Wright, in "Shaving," shares the bittersweet moment when he realized his father was no longer able to shave himself.

> *When his match, when his match kept missing*
> *his pipe . . .*

I invite you to sample the pleasure of reading poetry on a subject important to us all: having and raising children.

Bruce Lansky

FOREWORD

*Y*our children are not your children.
They are the sons and daughters of Life's longing for itself.
They come through you but are not from you,
and though they are with you, yet they belong not to you.

You may give them your love but not your thoughts,
for they have their own thoughts.
You may house their bodies but not their souls,
for their souls dwell in the house of tomorrow,
which you cannot visit, not even in your dreams.
You may strive to be like them,
    but seek not to make them like you.
For life goes not backward nor tarries with yesterday.

Kahlil Gibran

DANCING BABY

I felt you dance into me.
Oh, some babies are born
of hot, white passion;
others in a cool, momentary
indifference with untroubled sleep the
real reward.

But you danced in
with the moon waxed and
your daddy singing a love song
to the sky,
a song with my name and
yours ribboning through it
until there was a chain so
long, so strong, that
you had no choice but to
follow it, to join our joy,
to dance into my belly and
rest untroubled for
nine lovely months until you
were ready to sing your own
love song.

Laurie Lico Albanese

A Shower for My Son

Though you have
not yet come
from the warm cocoon,
I want you
to know what joy
your mother has found
nestled here among
the gossamer wings
of pastel tissue;
the yellow, blue,
and white papers
that hold blankets,
shawls, and teddy bears.
Her cheeks aglow
with tears,
she carefully opens
each package,
closes her eyes,
and holds
to her breast
the promise
of the gift
still to come.

Charles Ghigna

NINTH MONTH INVENTORY

We have a silk-lined bassinet;
we have two kinds of cribs
(one portable, one stay-at-home);
we have a hundred bibs.

We have a thousand diapers;
we have a rocking chair;
we have a tiny comb in case
the baby has some hair.

We have a baby carriage
and a car seat and a swing;
we have twelve baby bottles
and a prechilled teething ring.

We have ten books on baby care
and parenting techniques;
we have six rubber lap pads
in case the baby leaks.

We have three closets full of sheets
and blankets, towels, and clothes;
we have a baby-sized syringe
for cleaning out the nose.

We have a yellow rubber duck;
we have a soft brown teddy;
we have eleven charge cards
in case we're still not ready.

Leslie D. Perkins

• 4 •

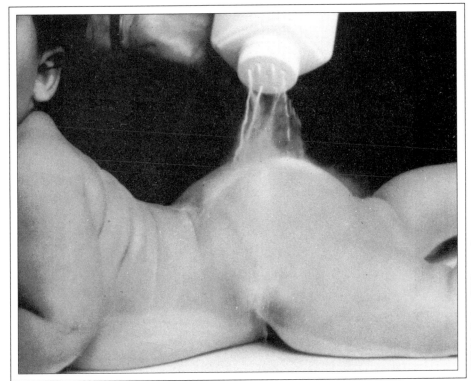

HAVING GIVEN BIRTH

For the first time,

my body comes back
to itself.

Stretch marks on my breasts
fade pale
as milk.

Around my head, songs
from my childhood quiver
like moths. They ask
to be taken back,
they ask forgiveness
for having been gone so long.

Through my own lips,
my mother's voice
sings my daughter to sleep.

When she sleeps
at my breast, I become
the oldest person
I have ever known.

I am younger than I can remember.

Ingrid Wendt

THE BABY

*T*he cat
who purrs
so sweetly
cannot fathom
why her place
in our bed
has been taken
by this one
who cries.

Susan Eisenberg

NEW DAUGHTER

Perfection, pure
and simple,
in miniature
with dimple.

Maureen Cannon

MINIATURE

*M*y day-old son is plenty scrawny,
his mouth is wide with screams, or yawny,
his ears seem larger than his needing.
His nose is flat, his chin receding,
his skin is very, very red,
he has no hair upon his head,
and yet I'm proud as proud can be
to hear you say he looks like me.

Richard Armour

MOVED

I move her,
baking in sunlight, into my shade.
Sleeping, she suckles an invisible breast
as if I were still attached,
still full of the sweetness
that fattened those cheeks, those thighs,
that flesh like kneaded dough, rising.
I marvel at her plumpness,
at myself for filling her so fully
with nothing more, no others needed;
I feed on *her* now.
She yawns, and as her eyes open,
she spoons a smile into my hungry heart
where it warms me like no oven.

Margaret Park Bridges

BREATHE DEEP

Whole-wheat bread
baking a crisp crust
on a December morning,

fresh-mown bluegrass
under the July sun,

hamburgers grilling
over a charcoal fire,

red clover
blooming
in a Kansas field,

apple muffins
split and steaming cinnamon
as the butter melts,

a Peace rose
in a crystal bowl
on my kitchen table;

my baby boy,
bathed and powdered,
cuddling against my cheek.

Life is full.
Just breathe
deep.

Sheryl Nelms

HEREDITY

*L*ike his father, an engineer,
Daniel turns his rattle over,
examines the construction, checks
the dynamics, admires the lines.
Suddenly, a gene from his
great-great-grandfather,
the French violinist, takes over.
        He waves the rattle
        up and down,
        to the right,
        to the left,
        straight ahead,
conducting an orchestra
from his high-chair podium.

Anita Gevaudan Byerly

NICE BABY

*L*ast year I talked about black humor and the impact of the common
        market on the European economy and
threw clever little cocktail parties in our discerningly eclectic
        living room
with the Spanish rug and the hand-carved Chinese chest and the
        Lucite chairs and
was occasionally hungered after by highly placed men in
        communications, but
this year we have a nice baby
and Pabulum drying on our Spanish rug,
and I talk about nursing versus sterilization
while men in communications
hunger elsewhere.

Last year I studied flamenco and had my ears pierced and
served an authentic fondue on the Belgian marble table of our
        discerningly eclectic dining area, but
this year we have a nice baby
and Spock on the second shelf of our Chinese chest,
and instead of finding myself I am doing my best
to find a sitter
for the nice baby banging the Belgian marble with his cup
while I heat the oven up
for the TV dinners.

Last year I had a shampoo and set every week and
slept an unbroken sleep beneath the Venetian chandelier of our
            discerningly eclectic bedroom, but
this year we have a nice baby,
and Gerber's strained bananas in my hair,
and gleaming beneath the Venetian chandelier,
a diaper pail, a Portacrib, and him,
a nice baby, drooling on our antique satin spread
while I smile and say how nice. It is often said
that motherhood is very maturing.

Judith Viorst

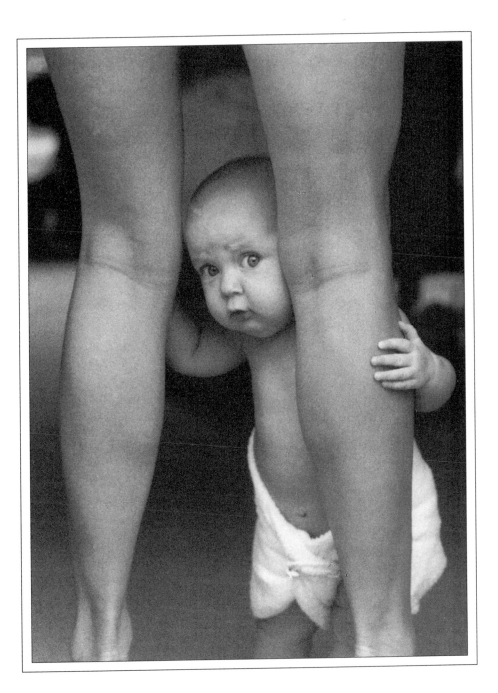

The Difference Is . . .

*F*irst-time parents never miss
a single tiny feat.
They film it,
note it in The Book,
and shout it on the street:
"He smiled today!
Had four BMs!
He spit up on the cat!
He got a tooth!
He slept all night—can you imagine that?"

But second-timers note the facts
and take each one in stride:
"He's learned to take his diaper off—
you'd better step aside."

Babs Bell Hajdusiewicz

FEASTING ON CRUMBS

All day, strapped in her stroller—
my two-year-old, not in control
of a single turn, a single stop
or go, or bumpy route pursued.
But now on the long stretch
of park grass, released, she runs
with purpose, in a perfect line
toward a flock of pigeons feasting
on crumbs, squeals with delight at
the explosion she creates—
her small arms in the air like a
sorceress—the beating of wings
above her, a snow of feathers all
around.
Finally, she has altered the world.

Robert Scotellaro

SMALL SONG FOR DADDY

*I*t isn't like my daughter
to awaken at one a.m.—
but here she is
wide-eyed and smiling.

She pulls the hairs on my chest
idly, wiggles her toes, sighs
almost as if in meditation,
and begins to sing softly,

the language hers alone,
the voice clear and fragile
as water striking stone.

New in a world where new
is all she knows, she sings
for each new wonder
she discovers—as if those

curtains, the chair, that
box of Kleenex were created
solely to delight her.

And they do. And she sings,
not knowing she is singing
for a father much in need
of her particular song.

W. D. Ehrhart

HIS TOYS

We planned to keep your first toys,
preserve them; one day,
when you were grown, lead you
to a secret closet, watch you
pull wide, amazed,
rediscover your treasures.
But we can't; you're eating them.

Michael Dennis Browne

ME TIME

I longed for morning quiet time—
an hour just for me.
So I got up at six o'clock,
but *me* time turned to *we:*

The dog woke up and wanted out;
my toddler heard the door.
And where was I at six-o-five
but playing on the floor.

The next day I got up at five;
my nine-month-old did, too.
And where was I at five-o-five
but playing peek-a-boo.

This morning I got up at four
and tip-toed 'round the house,
but squeaks he'd *never* heard before
aroused my amorous spouse.

No matter what I do or when,
I'm always up at bat.
They must think I'm a VIP . . .
I think I'll sleep on that.

Babs Bell Hajdusiewicz

IN LIEU OF WINGS

*I*n lieu of wings,
you rode my shoulders,
flapping your arms the
whole way to the playground—

so full of hope,
so full of vigor,
I thought we might both rise
up off the ground.

Robert Scotellaro

THE ABSENCE OF CROWS

*S*he is sitting at my desk,
writing a story about her life.
At age four, there is much to tell.

"I'll read you my story," she says,
decoding mysterious symbols.
"A big black crow

flew down and took a baby robin
out of her nest. Her Mom was gone,
she was looking for worms

for her baby to eat."
"That's a sad story," I say.
"The Mom had to be gone," she insists,

"she was looking for worms
for her baby to eat." Clumsy,
ready to plunge in, to explain

or lessen the trauma of tragic events,
I am interrupted. "That's not
the end of the story." She reads,

"The crow came back. He took
the other baby robin out of the nest."
(She turns over the page,

she has written on both sides.)
"The Mom was gone a long time,
she got lost and couldn't find worms."

She looks up from the nest,
squinting at the light on my desk.
I pray for the absence of crows.

Charlotte F. Otten

REVOLUTION

What time I spend with colored threads
replacing buttons Junior sheds!
And while I sew, I often rave
about the time that I could save
if children's buttons only grew
in neatly packaged sets of two,
with new ones ready underneath
to pop in place like second teeth.

Evelyn Amuedo Wade

CLARITY

*W*aking, Sophie at four asks, *How was the first person made?*
I tender a feeble story of sparks and water
that is no answer, so she decides *God must be real,*

while outside her window, wind stirs the valley
into wild country: basil and pepper plants
confuse new leaves with lunaria seed,
perfect stars of columbine fall in swallowtails,
and I realize the miracle
that she feels no need to stumble around in.
The word *God* can hold it. Perhaps it is her certainty

that she belongs here. In the garden now,
busy collecting what the wind has lost—
torn poppy, tiny catkins of pollen,
wine leaves of Japanese maple—
she dissembles the universe into its smallest syllables,
fits the mystery back into her hands.

Julia Levine

A HIDDEN WORLD

*H*ave you ever peeked into the opening
of an automatic teller machine,
or noticed how you look
in a doorknob or a spoon?
When was the last time you took a shortcut
to get home,
or watched pieces of dust
twirling in a sunbeam?
My son guides me through a world
otherwise hidden to me.

Betsy Franco

WAIT FOR ME!

"Mommy, wait for me!"
The cry pierced my busy mind,
and I paused . . .
realizing that once again
I had walked too fast,
remembering that children respond
instantly in wonder
to their world
and are not meant
to hustle.
Take your time, my child.
I will share your wonder
for a while.
My hurry only takes me faster
to the time
when I will walk too slow for you,
and you may hear my echo of your plea,
"Son, wait for me!"

Sylvia Andrews

I Know What Love Is

*T*ucked in the corner of my front porch,
hidden from the cool wind,
drinking in the autumn sun,
Becca sits as close as she can get,
eating her apple.

Her small mouth opens wide around the rosy flesh.
Her nose wrinkles with the effort of biting.
She knows I am watching and says,
"I love you, Mom."

How can I possibly want more
than a warm porch in the autumn sun
and sweet, rosy-skinned apples
to share with Becca?

Judi James

SONG FOR A DEAF CHILD

*Y*ou sit coiled in my lap,
a wound spring sleeping,

and in your dream
you hear the blue waters
rushing to sing to you,

and in your dream you know
what the grass is saying,
the birds, the trees,

and in your dream your ears
open like early flowers,
like parched lips

that drink in the words . . .
the words . . . the words
of all the world.

Margerie Goggin Allen

DAISY CHAIN OF LOVE

*M*y metropolitan daughter
picked some daisies
when she came
to visit the farm.
I placed them in fresh water,
and days on end
they held their heads high,
their golden centers
like genuine coins
that resisted tarnish.

They carry me back to another time.
I see her tiny fingers
clutching daisies,
holding them out.
I hear my little girl say,
"These are for you, Mommy."
That little crumpled bouquet
blooms as fresh and bright today
as these in the vase before me.

Faye Click

DYED IN THE WOOL

When filled with contentment,
the children and I
are gathered together
with eggs and with dye,
with transfers and crayons
and dubious skills,
I always forget about
possible spills.
But an egg is an object
so easy to slip,
and dye is a substance
so likely to drip.
It seeps in the carpet,
the splotches are bright,
and I scold just a bit,
but the kids are contrite.
I send them to bed
with a kiss and a hug.
The eggs are all finished—
and so is the rug.

Evelyn Amuedo Wade

DAVE'S READY

*T*he new clothes
are ready
and laid out.

The little rag rug
is bought.

He has all of the supplies
on the list:
    crayons,
    thick pencil #2,
    a Big Chief,
    rounded scissors,
    and glue,
all sacked up
to go.

It's all there.

He's met the teacher
and she's pretty.
He's seen his room.
They have hamsters
and guppies.

It will be fun,
he knows.

Now if I
can just let him
go.

Sheryl Nelms

Now Get Going

I send my daughters to school
like small packages
adorned with parts-missing jewelry
and pony stickers,
their fragrant hair tied
and wrapped in ribbons,
dresses too short and paint-splattered,
stockings darned with red and purple threads,
frayed sneakers flaunting new alphabet laces—
my proud, tiny bag ladies
dancing with excitement.
I want to mark them First Class
and Handle with Care.
I want to issue an all-points alert:
Be kind to them.
They travel in heart-shaped sunglasses
and milk mustaches,
and they're ready to believe
Anything.
My Lilliputian ambassadors,
my own, sweet reckonings.

Linda O'Brien

BLESSING

When I was a child, the last thing
before I left the house,
the last thing

before I went out
to the school bus was
my mother would kiss me.
She would leave a deep red
smear on my mouth
I would carry with me

into the bus, into the thick press
of bodies, damp woolen coats and boots
fresh from barns.

I would keep that kiss with me
long into the day, the taste
on my lips,

so if it seemed that I was too shy
to speak, or didn't know
answers, it's just that my mouth

was carefully holding its own
secret knowledge.

Reen Murphy

It's Been Five Days

*F*rom my pillow I can hear
my son. He is sick.
His breath ripples up his throat
and vibrates in his nose
before backing down.
I have gotten up each night
and burned my wrists on his face.
One night, when the temperature was just too high,
I pulled him from the bed,
forced him into the tub,
where he sat like a wounded cat,
too sick to fight me
but angry enough to snarl.
I soaked his hair and drenched his body
as he cried for me to stop.
I scrubbed him with the towel
and cried because I could not make him better.

Barbara Merchant

Rainy Day

*J*ust a newspaper article
about a little girl who saw her mother
knifed on a neighborhood street
and was left alone, sobbing in the rain
by the wilted, still-warm body,
is enough for me
to clutch the filthy pages in my fists,
shaking loudly next to strangers
on the five-fifteen commute,
my eyes overflowing useless dams.
Back home, I rush in
and grab you like a raincoat,
wrap your tiny arms around me and
inhale you with a sigh
that swells my heart until it hurts
and presses up against my ribs
like an opening umbrella.

Margaret Park Bridges

MY DAUGHTER'S EYES

*a*re the sea
upon which the ship
of all my dreams
sets sail.

Charles Ghigna

HARVEST

Two cherished bare spots
grace our lawn,
brown patches
shoes have scuffed upon.
From swinging fast,
then dragging slow,
these spots no grass
but children grow.

Lois Muehl

STAYING IN LINE

*B*ack before seat belts,
Dad sat me on his lap
and let me steer his '48 Packard
straight along the highway,
smooth as a hawk's flight.
I glided into our driveway,
fed the car easily
into our garage's narrow mouth.
I never saw his hands beneath mine
on the steering wheel,
smoothing the curves,
keeping us subtly and safely
on the straight road,
my father behind me all the way
with gentle nudging and secret steering,
keeping it all in line.

Gene Fehler

THANK GOODNESS FOR THE PICKLE JAR

*T*hank goodness for the pickle jar,
a standard feature in our car.
When sons have signaled they must go,
and traffic's jammed or lights are slow,
our handy-dandy pickle jar
relieves the tension where we are.
I can't imagine what folks do
when daughters need to potty, too.

Sydnie Meltzer Kleinhenz

FIRST JACK-O'-LANTERN

She picked the roundest one—
an eye for symmetry, for
spherical beauty.
Took the small knife (we cringed) and
labored like a sculptor, chipping
out a nose, then eyes—
an imperfect geometry of lopsided
triangles, an incapable square.
But for the mouth, she bit her
lip in concentration, fashioned
jagged teeth. Scowled and squinted—
her face a mask of mock evil.
Her fingers slippery with pulp.
And then, with a final cut, her
mask unhinged as she held up her
failed globe of malice—its kindly
eyes, its grin without a dark
infusion, her soul too bright.
Its silly cartoon face, later,
as the candle burned; its warm smile
lighting the porch.

Robert Scotellaro

MY SON SEASONS HIS MITT

The glove,
leather,
large as a plate,
his hand so small.
I want to tell him
curves can come
too fast and you
won't be ready.
Practice. Learn the game.
He rubs oil in,
kneading the roundness
like a shoulder,
rolls and ties
the glove around the ball.
How does he know? He's eight,
and no manual came with the mitt.
Some secret in his genes?
He sleeps with the new
glove oiled and leather
smelling brown
against his pillow.

I want for him
home runs,
impossible catches,
swift plays,
and slides into bases
so sure, the dust
doesn't notice.

Ruth Moose

IT'S LIKE A ZOO AT MEALTIME

My children ask for special foods
and I comply. Their list includes:
fresh apple cores and lettuce hearts,
unappetizing chicken parts,
raw nuts and seeds, and rock-hard bread,
some snails and fish—which all get fed
to critters who, instead of roam,
accompany my children home.

Sydnie Meltzer Kleinhenz

DRESS UP

The little girls are wearing
three skirts each,
blankets wrapped underneath
for hips. Looped
with shoelace bows,
sashed, festooned with tea-towel aprons,
plastic pearls, they dance
into the garden.
Leaves in their hair,
stolen bobby pins leak out
between their fingers.
"We're looking for flowers," they say,
giggling up to the lemon tree,
stuffing pairs of bulbous fruit
down their dress fronts.
They do not want me to see this.
They come back to the house,
arms folded before them,
spill into the smallest bedroom.
There they will take turns consulting
the mirror on the wall.

Robin Shectman

ELEGY FOR THE ELDEST DAUGHTER

When she was a child
of nine,
polio shriveled her.

She wanted,
she said,
before her death,
struggling to breathe,
trying to crawl
through the bars
on the hospital bed,
to dance with Fred Astaire.

And, because he took himself lightly,
as angels do,
who would be surprised,
wherever heaven is,
if that was how
she left her prison.

S. M. Eichner

35 / 10

Brushing out my daughter's dark
silken hair before the mirror,
I see the gray gleaming on my head,
the silver-haired servant behind her. Why is it,
just as we begin to go,
they begin to arrive, the fold in my neck
clarifying as the fine bones of her
hips sharpen? As my skin shows
its dry pitting, she opens like a small
pale flower on the tip of a cactus;
as my last chances to bear a child
are falling through my body, the duds among them,
her full purse of eggs, round and
firm as hard-boiled yolks, is about
to snap its clasp. I brush her tangled,
fragrant hair at bedtime. It's an old
story—the oldest we have on our planet—
the story of replacement.

Sharon Olds

THE EMERGING ADULT

He's reached a milestone in his growth—
a joy we both can share.
Now when I'm slow at cleaning clothes,
he's got *my* socks to wear.

Or when he wants to show school spirit,
wearing red and blue,
he lets me know he likes *my* sweatshirt,
"Thanks, Mom, this'll do."

And if he gets his sneakers wet,
he borrows *my* size eights,
then boards the bus. I wave and smile
(relieved that he'll be gone a while
so I can cruise the streets in style
upon *his* inline skates).

Sydnie Meltzer Kleinhenz

DADDY'S SLEEPING BEAUTY

She told me about her first kiss,
the way he tilted his head
to make the noses fit,
and she smiled with a smile
I had not seen before.
I thought of an earlier smile
on the face of a little girl
when Cinderella's slipper fit . . .
when Beauty turned her Beast into a prince . . .
when Rapunzel let down her golden hair. . . .
She hugged me and ran off to bed,
off to her dreams,
the dreams that might someday take her away.
As she closed the door, I knew that it was so.
What love it is that loves by letting go.

Brod Bagert

Sign for My Father Who Stressed the Bunt

On the rough diamond,
the hand-cut field below the dog lot and barn,
we rehearsed the strict technique
of bunting. I watched from the infield,
the mound, the backstop
as your left hand climbed the bat, your legs
and shoulders squared toward the pitcher.
You could drop it like a seed
down either base line. I admired your style,
but not enough to take my eyes off the bank
that served as our center-field fence.

Years passed, three leagues of organized ball,
no few lives. I could homer
into the garden beyond the bank,
into the left-field lot of Carmichael Motors,
and still you stressed the same technique,
the crouch and spring, the lead arm absorbing
just enough impact. The whole tiresome pitch
about basics never changing,
and I never learned what you were laying down.

Like a hand brushed across the bill of a cap,
let this be the sign
I'm getting a grip on the sacrifice.

David Bottoms

AT THE CROSSROADS

*T*onight I buy my son a mountain bike.
Independent of his father,
we pick a bicycle from a rack of wheels.
It's already assembled and has eighteen speeds,
more than an eleven-year-old needs.

George walks the bike out to the car but refuses
to let me carry it home in the trunk. He says
the frame will get nicked where the latch hits it.
I don't argue much, remembering how my ex-husband
gouged the cabinet on my new sewing machine
removing it from the van and how the scratch ruined
my pleasure every time I sewed.

It's dark now, but my son begs to ride home,
three miles from the shopping center.
I can't let him venture out alone like that,
not yet. We compromise. I accompany him,
monitor his progress along the route.
He takes off and I follow, track him like radar.
No parking allowed on the main street, so I forge ahead,
stop at parking lots and side streets to wait.

He takes longer than I think he should.
I know his father wouldn't approve,
would have hoisted the bike into the trunk and hauled it home,
made him wait another day to try his wheels.
I'd be home now instead of standing on an isolated corner,
peering down a dark corridor of trees for my son to emerge.
It's always been this way, me just ahead watching
my child clambering after, searching for me like a landmark.

At each junction he appears, weary and relieved.
Every day he pedals farther away from me,
and I sense the time approaching
when he won't need me to navigate the night with him,
like two bats squeaky as hinges at twilight;
but tonight he still looks for me at every intersection.
Just as much, I need to measure how much distance
I must put between us in order to stay this close.

Mary Harris

CHILDHOOD IS A CULTURE

Childhood is a culture of its own.
It has its own language,
its own rules,
its own rituals
and rites of passage.

When I'm tired
or preoccupied
and they are wrestling
on my newly made bed,
theirs can seem like a
primitive,
animalistic civilization,

and when I'm rested
and open
and we're saving worms
from rain puddles,
I feel privileged
to participate
in their native traditions.

Betsy Franco

SINGLE PARENTING

*I*t is not the big things.
Somehow, you always cope with those.
It is the little things that get you down.
There is no one to share the good times with,
the small moments of laughter.
No one to ask advice.
Is she old enough to "overnight"?
Is he too young to date?
Single is lonely at graduations,
parent teas, and conferences.
Single is scared when midnight comes
and he isn't home from a movie date,
or she has a boyfriend too old, too wise.
Single is carrying alone
a burden meant to be shared.

Joyce Freeman-Clark

From "Thinking about My Father"

I have no memory of his
holding me as an infant,
but we have an old home
movie in which my twenty-
two-year-old mother walks
out onto the front porch
and hands a baby to this
thin young man. Some days
I wake up limp and happy
as that child, smiled at
and lifted up to the sun
by someone who wanted me
right here in this world.

David Huddle

THREE TEENAGERS

*T*oday it was

pack a diet sack lunch for Julie,
then drive her to work
because her car is in the shop,

hurry home in time
to fix dinner
for Ben and Dave,

then drive Ben to work
because he doesn't have a car yet,

stopping by the bank
to cash four graduation checks for Julie
and a tax refund for Ben
on my way to pick up Julie,

going by the Chevy garage
to check on her car
that isn't done yet,

finally getting home

to pick up Dave
to take him to get a haircut,
after I take him
by the library
on our way to get his
job application
at Skaggs,

squeezing in
supper

before I have to pick up Ben.

And people wonder
what I do with all my time,
now that my kids are
nearly grown.

Sheryl Nelms

Excerpt from a Letter to Rebecca

I can read your mind
every time that wry smile
crosses your face.
Daddy, you are thinking,
will never change.
You are right, of course.
Daddy is a stone skimming surfaces
for fear of depths beneath.
From the old school,
he is a compulsive doer
in subconscious control, not knowing
how to just be, to sit occasionally
in silence, maybe
even take my hand a while.
Well, you've heard that story
all your life. What he can't tell you,
mute in his masculine jail,
is that he loves who you have become,
but still longs for the child
who snuggled against him
each bedtime
as he read for the thousandth time
Green Eggs and Ham,
both of you
knowing every word by heart.

Margerie Goggin Allen

THE STAGGER

*T*he staggered start makes him
seem behind when the gun
goes off. He is slow to
rise from his crouch and hits
full stride well after all
the others. But I have
faith now in his power,
showing itself as he
moves at his own sure pace.

I love to see my son
running the turn, making
up the stagger before
the straightaway. He leans
in, slack-faced, knees lifting,
claiming the inside lane
with his natural speed.

In his seventeenth year,
when I least expected
it, he has given me
a way to see him leave
childhood clear. There is no
tension in his body
as the finish line nears.
He sees it and maintains
good form, running as if
there were no tape to break.

Floyd Skloot

DANCE OF THE DARKROOM

At the high-school sock hop, Johnny and I
sneaked away from our dates to the darkroom
next to the physics lab where Mr. Brooks kept his radio.
Music from the gym seeped through old floorboards;
too softly, though, to drown out the NCAA basketball
championship play-by-play of LaSalle-Iowa,
sweeter to my ears than any love song.

If our dates missed us on the dance floor
that hour or so, they never said.
But to Mom's question, "How was the dance?"
I grinned and said in truth, "The best ever."
There's no way she could hide her sudden smile.
I knew how happy she was at the progress
being made by her son, the wallflower.

Gene Fehler

DAUGHTER

*W*here mother failed to make a lady of me
(dutiful, well-groomed, always polite)—
found fault with all I did, with all I was,
quick-tongued and rational, sure she was right—

my daughter may succeed. It stands to reason:
love has a more enticing sound than duty,
and those young eyes that overlook my flaws
create in me something akin to beauty.

That child who grew to be what I was not,
more like myself than I could ever be,
has always had my love, has had my pride,
and now gives back my self, intact, to me.

Laughing and mischievous, we play a game
that has no penalties, no fouls, no blame.

Elizabeth Bolton

THE VISIT

My son comes home for five days,
slipping back into the womb
smooth as water;
he drives me to market,
to malls, to doctors,
reaches shelves too high for me,
calls me *Ma*.
I iron his shirts, ask if he is
hungry, has he slept well,
listen for sounds
between the lines.
Today he slips out again,
right past my arms,
holding pot roast and cookies.

Dorothy Brummel

ADVICE FROM THE PAST

I never knew
my Mother's words
which I thought dull,
didactical,
would prove in time,
as decades sped,
so right, so sound,
so practical!

Lois Muehl

FOR A SON IN THE PERSIAN GULF

In the sixties, a huge glass peace sign
hung on the beam in our living room.
We didn't allow you to have toy guns or G. I. Joes.
Your best friend was a girl. You went fishing together,
sold lemonade on hot afternoons.
I showed you how to make origami cranes,
sent you to your room if you hit your brother.
Once, when I found you in the backyard,
staring down at the frog you'd killed,
I made you bury it and say a prayer.

Now I worry that you don't have the killer instinct,
that you'll be standing in the desert somewhere
and there will be that second
when you look away from the enemy line
and up at the sky, at the clouds I taught you to name.

Forgive me. I raised you for peace.

Sondra Upham

THE PARENT-POET AT FIFTY

When I am old
and wearing fuchsia polka dots,
I want them to say
not "She lived a long life,"
or even "A good life,"
but "She lived her own life."

It wasn't easy with
Phyllis Schlafly and Dr. Spock and
Gloria Steinem and Dr. Ruth
trying to live it for me.

There were times
when I wanted to hand it over:
"Scrub some floors, Gloria,
so I can have glorious sex
as Dr. Ruth prescribes
(you can rock the baby while I'm going at it);
and Ben can finish my novel
while breastfeeding on demand."

I figured Phyllis would lend a hand
as soon as she got back from her latest trip.
(I've always wondered how her family fared
while she was out of town telling me to stay at home.)

When I am old,
don't call me for dinner:
I'll be on the beach
with my grandchildren,
wetting my long skirts
and hearing the Atlantic roar through a seashell.

Karen Hammond

LULLABY FOR MY MOTHER

At night I make her bed
in the folds of old age.
Her skinny hand
pulls mine into the dark.

Before her dreams begin,
from a brain erased of speech,
a small cracked voice calls *mama,*
and I become my mother's mother
and am jolted
as if the earth's axis tilted
and the poles reversed.
Where am I?
I have no time for speculations.

Flustered, I wipe her dry
just as she once taught me.
Mama, she whispers,
worried at being naughty.
A draft streams in from the window.

Heating pad. Glass. The pills.
I tip the lampshade back.
Mama, don't leave me alone
all by myself in the dark.

She chokes her sobs
as I take her in my arms
so heavy with pain and fear.
She or me? In cold winter
a double cradle breaks.

Please wake me early.
I need an early start.
Is there anything left to do?
Which of us left work undone?

Mama, my child, sleep.
"Little baby bunting. . . ."

Blaga Dimitrova
Translated by John Balaban

SHAVING

When his match, when his match kept missing
his pipe, I knew from my father's face,
sharp gray stubs in a cornfield reaped and dry,
he hadn't begun a beard out of an old man's right,
or November whimsy, but that his hands were going.
Watching him there fumbling the light again,
I went back to another Sunday with him,
when on small boy's legs I fell behind him
in the snow going to church. He came back for me,
laughing, and boosted me to his chest. My cheeks
touched then two smoothnesses at once:
the velvet collar of his Lord Chesterfield
and the warm plains of his best Sunday face.

I lit his pipe and said, "Smoke that while I shave you
for Sunday." He sat on the toilet like
a good boy, taking medicine. My fingers
touched through the lather the cleft of his chin,
and the blade made pink and blue swaths
in the snowy foam, and we were done.
Pretending to test, I bent down my cheek to his
a moment, and then we went to church.

Charles David Wright

Contributor Notes and Acknowledgments

Laurie Lico Albanese is a well-anthologized poet with a national reputation. "Dancing Baby" copyright © by Laurie Lico Albanese. Excerpted with permission from *Mothering*, Volume #65. For subscriptions contact *Mothering*, PO Box 1690, Santa Fe, NM 87504. All rights reserved.

Margerie Goggin Allen was born in Massachusetts in 1927 and has a BFA from the Rhode Island School of Design. She currently lives in North Carolina with her husband. They have three daughters, one of whom died of cancer in 1967. "Song for a Deaf Child" and "Excerpt from a Letter to Rebecca" are copyright © 1994 by Margerie Goggin Allen.

Sylvia Andrews was born and educated in Northern Ireland, where she taught elementary school. She currently writes and teaches in Florida, where she lives with her husband, a teenage son, and a cat. "Wait for Me!" is copyright © 1994 by Sylvia Andrews.

Richard Armour is a famous, well-anthologized author of poetry for children and adults. "Miniature" copyright © by Richard Armour. From *For Partly Proud Parents* (Harper and Brothers, 1946). Reprinted with permission of Kathleen Armour.

Brod Bagert is a husband, the father of four children, a former trial-lawyer and New Orleans City Councilman, and a poet who writes for child and adult audiences. "Daddy's Sleeping Beauty" copyright © 1992 by Brod Bragert. Reprinted with permission of the author.

Elizabeth Bolton, born in New York City, now lives in Oregon. The author of over fifty published poems, she holds a BA from Pomona College and an MA from Penn State. "Daughter" copyright © 1994 by Elizabeth Bolton.

David Bottoms is a widely anthologized poet and a professor of English at Georgia State University. "Sign for My Father Who Stressed the Bunt" copyright ©1983 by David Bottoms. From *In a U-Haul, North of Damascus* published by William Morrow and Company, Inc., New York. Reprinted by permission of Maria Carvainis Agency, Inc. All rights reserved.

Margaret Park Bridges was born in 1957 in New York and raised in Oregon. She holds a BA in English from Bowdoin College and lives in Massachusetts with her husband and two daughters. "Moved" and "Rainy Day" copyright © 1994 by Margaret Park Bridges.

Michael Dennis Browne was born in 1940 in England. A graduate of the Iowa Writer's Workshop, he currently lives in Minneapolis with his wife, a son, and two daughters. "His Toys" copyright © 1994 by Michael Dennis Browne.

Dorothy Brummel was born and raised in New York, and now lives in Florida with her husband. They have two adult sons. "The Visit" copyright © 1994 by Dorothy Brummel.

Anita Gevaudan Byerly was born in Pittsburgh in 1929. As a single parent, she raised a son and a daughter while working as a secretary before returning to college and earning a BA from the University of Pittsburgh. She has four grandchildren. "Heredity" copyright © 1994 by Anita Gevaudan Byerly.

Maureen Cannon is a widely anthologized poet with a national reputation. "New Daughter" copyright © by Maureen Cannon. Reprinted with permission of the author.

Joyce Freeman-Clark was born in Oregon in 1931. After raising her own family, she returned to college, graduating from SOSC in 1989 with two BS degrees, one in history, one in education. She has seven children, twelve grandchildren, and two great-grandchildren. "Single Parenting" copyright © 1994 by Joyce Freeman-Clark.

Faye Click was born in Kentucky, earned BS and MA degrees from Eastern University, and currently lives in Richmond with her husband. They are the parents of three adult children. "Daisy Chain of Love" copyright © 1994 by Faye Click.

Blaga Dimitrova is one of the foremost poets of Bulgaria, where she recently served as Vice President in that country's new government. Her translator, *John Balaban,* is the author of nine books of poetry, prose, and translation. "Lullaby for My Mother" by Blaga Dimitrova. First appeared in *Poets of Bulgaria* (Unicorn Press). Copyright © this translation John Balaban 1988.

W. D. Ehrhart was born in 1948 in Pennsylvania. An ex–Marine sergeant and Vietnam veteran, he now lives in Philadelphia with his wife and daughter. "Small Song for Daddy" by W. D. Ehrhart. Reprinted from *Just for Laughs* by W. D. Ehrhart, Viet Nam Generation, Inc., & Burning Cities Press, 1990, and with permission of the author.

S. M. Eichner is a retired college professor. She has taught writing skills in poetry, fiction, and the essay to many college students and adults. "Elegy for the Eldest Daughter" copyright © 1994 by S. M. Eichner.

Susan Eisenberg is a widely published poet with a national reputation. "The Baby" copyright © 1984 by Susan Eisenberg. Reprinted with permission of the author. First appeared in *In Celebration of Babies* (Ballantine, 1987).

Gene Fehler was born in 1940 in Illinois, earned an MS from Northern Illinois University, and has authored over 600 poems. He currently lives in South Carolina with his wife. They have two grown sons. "Staying in Line" and "Dance of the Darkroom" copyright © 1994 by Gene Fehler.

Betsy Franco was born in 1947 in Ohio and writes children's books and educational materials. She lives in northern California with her husband and her three sons. "A Hidden World" and "Childhood Is a Culture" copyright © 1994 by Betsy Franco.

Charles Ghigna is a poet and children's author. His books include *Father Goose, Speaking in Tongues,* and Pulitzer Prize-nominee *Returning to Earth.* He lives in Alabama with his wife and son. "A Shower for My Son" and "My Daughter's Eyes" copyright © 1994 by Charles Ghigna.

Kahlil Gibran is famous for his long poem-story, *The Prophet.* "Foreword" excerpted from *The Prophet* by Kahlil Gibran. Copyright © 1923 by Kahlil Gibran and renewed 1951 by Administrators C.T.A. of Kahlil Gibran Estate and Mary G. Gibran. Reprinted by permission of Alfred A. Knopf, Inc.

Babs Bell Hajdusiewicz was born in 1944 in Indiana. The author of more than 60 books and 250 poems for children, she founded "Booking the Future," a community-based national literacy program. She lives in Houston with her husband, and a son and a daughter, both teenagers. "Me Time" and "The Difference Is . . ." copyright © 1994 by Babs Bell Hajdusiewicz.

Karen Hammond was born in Massachusetts and holds an MA from SUNY-Binghamton. A professional writer for over twenty years, she also teaches advanced writing at SUNY-Binghamton. "The Poet-Parent at Fifty" copyright © 1994 by Karen Hammond.

Mary Harris was born in Chicago in 1952 but grew up in southern California. She currently lives in Ventura, California, where she works for the *Star-Free Press*. She is the mother of one teenage son. "At the Crossroads" copyright © 1994 by Mary Harris.

David Huddle, a widely anthologized poet, lives in Vermont. "Thinking about My Father" by David Huddle first appeared in *The Kenyon Review* (Fall, 1990) and later in *The Nature of Yearning* (Gibbs Smith, Publisher, 1992). Reprinted by permission of the author.

Judi James was born in 1958 in Wisconsin, where she currently lives with her husband and their three daughters. "I Know What Love Is" copyright © 1994 by Judi James.

Sydnie Meltzer Kleinhenz likes to laugh about life, being forty, and raising five sons with their rodents, reptiles, and amphibians. Originally from Missouri, she now lives in Texas with her husband and their sons. "Thank Goodness for the Pickle Jar," "It's Like a Zoo at Mealtime," and "The Emerging Adult" copyright © 1994 by Sydnie Meltzer Kleinhenz.

Julia Levine is a widely anthologized poet with a national reputation. "Clarity" by Julia Levine. Excerpted with permission from *Mothering*, Volume #69. For subscriptions contact *Mothering*, PO Box 1690, Santa Fe, NM 87504. All rights reserved.

Barbara Merchant was born in 1960 in Alabama, holds an AB from the University of Alabama, and currently lives in Georgia with her two sons. "It's Been Five Days" copyright © 1994 by Barbara Merchant.

Ruth Moose is the author of two poetry collections, *To Survive* and *Finding Things in the Dark*. She teaches at Pfieffer College in North Carolina and is married to a visual artist with whom she has raised two sons. "My Son Seasons His Mitt" copyright © 1994 by Ruth Moose.

Lois Muehl was born in Illinois in 1920. She received a BA from Oberlin College and an MA from the University of Iowa. She currently lives in Iowa with her husband, with whom she has raised a daughter and three sons, two of whom are twins. "Harvest" and "Advice from the Past" copyright © 1994 by Lois Muehl.

Reen Murphy was born in Minnesota in 1947 and holds two bachelor degrees from Moorhead State University. Reen currently lives in Fergus Falls, Minnesota, with her husband. They have three teenage children. "Blessing" copyright © 1994 by Reen Murphy.

Sheryl Nelms was born in 1944 in Kansas and hold a BS from South Dakota State University. She is the author of over 3,000 published poems, short stories, and articles. She now lives in Texas with her husband, two sons, and a daughter. "Three Teenagers," "Dave's Ready," and "Breathe Deep" copyright © 1994 by Sheryl Nelms.

Linda O'Brien is a well-anthologized poet with a national reputation. "Now Get Going" by Linda O'Brien. Excerpted with permission from *Mothering*, Volume #62. For subscriptions contact *Mothering*, PO Box 1690, Santa Fe, NM 87504. All rights reserved.

Sharon Olds was born in 1942 in San Francisco and educated at Stanford University and Columbia University. The author of several award-winning collections of poetry, she teaches at New York University. "35/10" copyright © 1983 by Sharon Olds. Originally appeared in *The Dead and the Living* (1984). Reprinted by permission of Alfred A. Knopf and the author.

Charlotte F. Otten is a professor of English literature at Calvin College in Michigan. Her poems have appeared in many periodicals and she has also written a book of children's poems scheduled for 1994. "The Absence of Crows" copyright © 1994 by Charlotte F. Otten.

Leslie D. Perkins was born in Florida in 1953. She has a BA in English from Carleton College and writes picture books and poetry. She currently lives in California with her husband and a daughter. "Ninth Month Inventory" copyright © 1994 by Leslie D. Perkins.

Robert Scotellaro was born and raised in Manhattan, spent a tour of duty in Vietnam, then moved to San Francisco where he currently lives with his wife. He is the father of two daughters. "Feasting on Crumbs," "First Jack-o'-Lantern," and "In Lieu of Wings" copyright © 1994 by Robert Scotellaro.

Robin Shectman was born in Ohio in 1948 but raised in suburban New York City. She now lives in southern California with her husband, an astronomer. They have two adult children. "Dress Up" copyright © 1994 by Robin Shectman.

Floyd Skloot was born in Brooklyn in 1947. He earned an MA from Southern Illinois University. He is the father of two adult children, a son and a daughter. He currently lives in Oregon with his wife. "The Stagger" copyright © 1994 by Floyd Skloot.

Sondra Upham was born in Nebraska in 1942 and holds degrees from Gustavus Adolphus and the University of Nebraska. She is currently pursuing a master's degree at the University of Massachusetts in Boston. "For a Son in the Persian Gulf" copyright © 1993 by Sondra Upham. Originally appeared in *We Speak for Peace* (1993). Reprinted by permission of the author.

Judith Viorst is a nationally recognized poet whose most recent credit is the novel *Murdering Mr. Monti* (1994). "Nice Baby" copyright © 1968 by Judith Viorst. Originally appeared in *When Did I Stop Being Twenty and Other Injustices,* published by Simon & Schuster. Reprinted by permission of the author.

Evelyn Amuedo Wade, born in New Orleans, is a professor emeritus at Northern Virginia Community College and a poetry instructor at American University. She has published over 1,000 poems, is the mother of two sons and two foster children, and has five grandchildren. "Revolution" and "Dyed in the Wool" copyright © 1994 by Evelyn Amuedo Wade.

Ingrid Wendt was born in 1944 in Illinois and received an MFA from the University of Oregon. She has taught children, K-12, and has been a visiting professor at several universities. She lives in Oregon with her husband; they have one adult daughter. "Having Given Birth" copyright © 1994 by Ingrid Wendt.

Charles David Wright is a well-published, nationally recognized poet. "Shaving" is reprinted from *Early Rising,* by Charles David Wright. Chapel Hill: The University of North Carolina Press, 1968. Used by permission of the publisher.

Photo Credits

p. vi "A Blessing from Above" © 1994 by Nancy Kimball.

p. 5 © 1983 Robert Kaufman. All rights reserved.

p. 9 © 1994 Kathy Sloane.

p. 13 © Rod Mann.

p. 17 © 1988 by Dave Evans. Appeared in *Baby, Baby, Sweet Baby* by Bruce Velick (Pomegranate Publishing).

p. 20 © Association des Amis de Jacques-Henri Lartigue. Appeared in *Baby, Baby, Sweet Baby* by Bruce Velick (Pomegranate Publishing).

p. 25 © The Stock Market/Paul Barton 1990.

p. 30 © Kathryn Abbe.

p. 34 © 1979 by Bambi Peterson Anderson.

p. 41 © 1992 Ulrike Welsch. All rights reserved.

p. 44 "Girl in Window" © by Bill Ray.

p. 47 © Bill Binzen.

p. 50 © 1994 H. Armstrong Roberts.

p. 55 © Maggie Merkow.

p. 61 © 1987 by Geoffrey Clifford.

p. 65 "Children at Play, Cherry Plain, NY" © 1968 by Lilo Raymond.

p. 70 "The Little Prince" © 1988 by Marcia Lippman.

p. 74 © by Laura McPhee: Ringoes, New Jersey, 1984.

p. 78 © by Reuters/Bettmann.

p. 84 © 1990 Kent Reno/Jeroboam, Inc.

Meadowbrook Press would like to thank the following people for their help in selecting the poems which appear in this anthology:

Margerie Goggin Allen, Polly Andersen, Susan D. Anderson, Sylvia Andrews, Phil Bolsta, Elizabeth Bolton, Margaret Park Bridges, Dorothy Howe Brooks, Bill Brown, Sonja Brown, Dorothy Brummel, Anita Gevaudan Byerly, Marsh Cassady, Joyce Freeman-Clark, Faye Click, Larry Cohen, Barbara Crooker, Eileen Daily, Mary Collins Dunne, W. D. Ehrhart, S. M. Eichner, Gene Fehler, Betsy Franco, Greg Geleta, Charles Ghigna, Connie Jordan Green, Goldie Olsyznko Gryn, Babs Bell Hajdusiewicz, Karen Hammond, K. S. Hardy, Mary Harris, Dick Hayman, Joan Holleman, Judi James, Beatrice L. Jones, Jo S. Kittinger, Sydnie Meltzer Kleinhenz, Kim Koehler, Marilyn Krysl, Vicki McKinney, Jean H. Marvin, Barbara Merchant, Gwen Molnar, Ruth Moose, Lois Muehl, Reen Murphy, Sheryl Nelms, Lorraine Bates Noyes, Kathy Mosdal O'Brien, Charlotte Otten, Cynthia Pederson, Leslie D. Perkins, Claire Puneky, Jane Schapiro, Lawrence Schimel, Brad Schreiber, Robert Scotellaro, Jacqueline Seewald, Robin Shectman, Audrey Sherins, Floyd Skloot, Susan Rose Simms, Linda Torres, Esther Towns, Sondra Upham, Lisa Loeb Vittone, Evelyn Amuedo Wade, Penny Warner, Ingrid Wendt, Stan Lee Werlin, Charyl K. Zehfus, Steve Zweig.